UNDER A CIRCUS MOON

P O E M S

CATHERINE MCLAUGHLIN

Old Seventy Creek Press, 2015

ACKNOWLEDGMENTS

The poems below have been published in the following literary journals:

"All That Fall": *Southern Review*, Vol. 29 No. 3, Summer 1993; *Slant*, Summer 1993

"Analysis": *National Forum, Journal of Phi Kappa Phi*, Vol. LXXIV, No 1, Winter 1994

"Blue Collars": *Cream City Review*, Vol. 17 No 1. Spring 1993

"Instinct": *Commonweal*, Vol CXXI, No 9, 6 May 1994

"Katrinka and the Apple" (formerly "Child Abuse"): *National Forum, Journal of Phi Kappa Phi*, Vol LXXIV, No 2, Spring 1994

"Katrinka re-enters her life at a mid-point" (formerly "She re-enters her life at a mid-point"): *Midland Review*, June 1994

"Leaving Home": *Curbside Review*, Spring, 2006

"New England Reincarnation": *Ocean Voices Anthology*, Everett Hoagland, Ed., Spinner Publications, 2013

"Notes on Neurosis": *Psychopoetica*, Vol 211, 1991
"Some Women": *National Forum, Journal of Phi Kappa Phi*, Vol 75 No 1, Winter 1995

"Souvenirs": *Rhino*, 1993; *Ocean Voices Anthology*, Everett Hoagland, Ed., Spinner Publications, 2013

"Transition": *Southern Review,* Spring/Summer, 2004

"Water of Her Life": *Ocean Voices Anthology*, Everett Hoagland, Ed., Spinner Publications, 2013

"What I Am Trying to Tell You": *Wisconsin Review*, Vol 27 No 1, October 1992.

Furthermore, I wish to acknowledge the following people to whom a great debt is owed for their constant, unconditional support and encouragement:

My late and greatly loved mentors: James Baldwin, Robert Cormier, and Mary Mattfield;
The women of Women's Week: Sue Hayes, Susan McLeavy, and Rosemary Quinn;
And: Ayaan Agane, Marisa Allegra, Elaine Beilin, Everett Hoagland, Bernard Horn, Kathy Knutsen, Desmond McCarthy, Lynn Parker, Armand Viera, and Sam Witt.

Every word I write echoes your voices, true, honest, full-throated: they cradled me, sang me to sleep, comforted the dark nights, propped up my days, and bandaged my wounds. And oh! how we harmonized and laughed in the ocean, and talked until dawn.

CM
August 2015

DEDICATION

To my children, Conor-the-Photographer and Cate-the-Poet—
To my parents, Mary and Charlie Ouimet, deceased, though I never have been able to say goodbye—
To my siblings, Mary Elaine Viera, Kevin, Charles, and Christopher Ouimet, my life-blood, I have tried to be your voices, in harmony.

OLD SEVENTY CREEK PRESS FIRST EDITION
PRINTED IN THE UNITED STATES OF AMERICA
ALL RIGHTS RESERVED UNDER INTERNATIONAL
AND PAN-AMERICAN COPYRIGHT CONVENTIONS
PUBLISHED IN THE UNITED STATES
BY OLD SEVENTY CREEK PRESS
RUDY THOMAS, PUBLISHER
P. O. BOX 204
ALBANY, KENTUCKY 42602
ISBN-13: 978-0692527238 (Old Seventy Creek Press)
ISBN-10: 0692527230

UNDER A CIRCUS MOON

A few words about Under A Circus Moon

This powerful and accomplished collection has the force of vivid snapshots from a novel that reveals the whole life of a complex, ethical, and wise woman. At its heart is a series of fourteen poems in which the poet adopts a persona, Katrinka, to bravely and honestly reveal the lifelong consequences of childhood trauma. For the persona, the poet, and the reader, McLaughlin shows how "what burned yesterday returns alas/to burn again though with a different quality/of illumination lighting those dark corners/of an immutable shame."

Bernard Horn, author of **our daily words,** and other works. Bernie was the winner of the 2009 Old Seventy Creek Poetry Prize.

TABLE OF CONTENTS

Contents   Continued

BLUE COLLARS

Outside Providence
in a jumble of mill towns, bricks and turrets,
bars, diners and State Line Scrap
surround rows of triple deckers.
In a third floor tenement
a woman dressed in black, dark hair greying,
dusts gilt-edged bric-a-brac in glass closets
and the framed bleeding heart of Jesus
nailed to the wall. The daughter
sits under the slanted eaves on a bed
layered with handmade patchwork quilts,
a frayed afghan across her shoulders,
writing a language her mother cannot comprehend
and rarely speaks, the shape of new words
too sharp against the soft palate
of age and the old world.

The hall smells of spice and sausage,
but outside the air tingles with the promise of snow.
In that hour after the sun, before the moon,
schoolboys play ball against brick walls
suffused with pink and purple shadow.
Red-cheeked, blood stirred with vague longings,
they laugh and curse and yell in vibrant chorus
delighting in their strong limbs and raucous company.

From church to church the deep bells reverberate
and the men released from work appear,
lunch pails, caps and cigarettes.
The mother, sighing, rises to fix the family supper,
the tower clocks of the mills tell the hour,
steeple, chain and spire.

"ALL THAT FALL"

—Samuel Beckett

All that fall wind rattled trees
and slipped in keening through cracks in windows
or wherever insulation was weak,
and even through empty keyholes
it whistled in the dark and in the daytime whispered
ne pas encore, ne pas encore
through vacant chambers of the heart.

Colors changed in subtle ways to undramatic browns;
leaves fell in clumps from a lashing rain
or flew wind-thrust at windows
striking like small brown bats against the panes.

And I have seen them gather
huddled and possessive around the weathered stones,
heard them chatter,
mocking the very trunks that gave them life,
hissing at the bones of branches bared to the world

while others trapped in corners like lost chances
crumbled
into the soft brown dust of nevers.

All that fall lose touch
and sense that dizzying downward tumble
blown by raw blind ache
the densest need untended and unnamable.

ANALYSIS

Knowing what it is and where
precise as laser aimed at grey matter
the careful naming of winterlight
cautious probing into conscience and psyche
the whole crazy complex an Escher design
baffling synapses:
                    You set paths inside
out, offer street signs, signal
what I dare not guess.
I would rather pluck my truths
like apples from straight-rowed orchards;
you know this. It is why
when you send me back to navigate again
among the tortured fallow roots
your voice softens. Against
such gentleness there is no defense.

So here is the shoebox full of sand dollars,
bone-white fragility wrapped in layered tissue,
this house built of matchsticks,
a pair of skates with broken laces,
sounds of old blades scraping over new ice,
fragments of speech numbed by February air.

The late afternoon's undone
by shavings flung into a shaft of light.
Hunched in that old overcoat amid the dark things
wary and silent
the pain rests.

WHAT I AM TRYING TO TELL YOU

Why disturb this sleep
this subterranean wandering among saw-toothed fossils
reading the past stretched out in *bas-relief* by Braille
glossing over with facile touch
the tracings of trouble to trouble?
Would you have me give it all over
for the formless now? I have no words
for the present tense, only
unpicked peaches plumping off branches
to slowly fall one by one onto the spongy grass below,
only
crafty passive constructions and the split infinitives
that mark the pathology of language:

when floodgates open
all vestiges of civilization get washed away,
so many houses never with foundations of real account
tumbling in the mud,
so much lucidity lost
in the hollow repetition of sounds.

I know the hand planted between the shoulder
blades and the voice whispering from those old stones
are not yours. And I have learned that to truly touch, to feel
is to lie with your eyes shut
and everything else open to the dark.

What I am trying to tell you
is paradox:
when the heart in hibernation wakes,

blinking at the misaligned stars flung in unfamiliar
patterns, starved, desperate,
and caged of its own design,
it will devour itself.

PANIC ATTACK

Daydreaming the nightmare
of losing your mind----

soap in the butter dish
Cheerios awash in orange juice
phones jangling of missed appointments
and lost opportunities, or
the dread silence on the line
before the dial tone----

of winding up wound,
catatonic
when the kids return from school:
they will find you mute with possible disasters,
your heart gone wild
with the ceaseless pulsing of adrenaline
rushing, with nowhere to go, through infinite loops,
and mistake the sweat confounding your eyes
for the tears you've been unable to shed,
the glazed inability
to apprehend neither the end of it all
nor the beginning

INSTINCT

That cat flying its hull,
hellbent into the wind,
foams its own steep wake,
but only
because the sails strain against the sailor
who leans, stretching sinew, farther out
backward to danger,
a taut torso riding on air
flayed by salt
trusting only
the line she clings to.

NOTES ON NEUROSES

New England born and Irish bred
what could be but conscience
caught between lunacy and the neap tide?
No wonder, then, I was drawn to your eyes,
so intimate with the sea in small deaths and depth,
memories jagged as broken shells.

At night in the room walls fall away
grief settles in like a thick fog
where you recede and merge
we ride the hours like fishermen in curraghs
waiting for the great wave
that yet may break over the open boat
snapping its shell of skin drawn taut across bone:
there is salt spray on our cheeks.

By dawn
vague shapes solidify and state their names
while you rise and leave without speaking:
each morning we winkle each other out,
while every night we shell our souls.

WATER OF HER LIFE

She dreams of water, the imprint
of her infancy, the water of her baptism.
She dreams that cold Atlantic of her drowning once
in another life, the ice where life's breath
had formed around her mouth,
of life-vested bodies bobbing among the sea's debris—

She dreams of the time the ocean moved inland
the seawater dammed in her street, the boats
floating past parked Plymouths in 1954
and then the dikes built to protect the mills
long flat-topped hills of stone
her youthful shortcut to the beach—

She dreams of the Caribbean island
life source to carry her through midlife
the water of her womb gone dry
where once it nurtured four lives
and two survived the transition into air;
She is at one with salt, sea creatures and anemones,
shells and conches, and catamarans
the wild tilting of the world,
the port hull flying through the cerulean sea—

She dreams and in her dreams she hears
the squawking gulls, the mourning of the foghorn,
the wind, tasting of salt and smelling of the sea
the rubber from the Goodyear plant—

Water of her life, ever churning;
a brother lies drowning in his own fluid.
Helpless, forced by time and the tides of circumstance

to live inland, she longs only to return
to their watery beginnings
in the city of New Bedford
where the dreaming all began.

LEAVING HOME

You could hear the loss
in the sound of a spoon rattling a teacup
as my mother, at 80, drinks in the empty kitchen
this the only expression
for a silenced voice, silent with the weight of years,
the heft of unsaid goodbye to the tenement
of her childhood, and mine, and my children's—
I look to the sentiment
in boxes and plastic bags, the old chairs with worn-
down arms,
tables scratched with our growing pains,
on a wall
inside my old closet, my father's whimsical sketch of
Kilroy
will not be erased with spray and scrubbing,
and there
the wide patch of plaster of Paris covering the hole
I'd nightly pick at to reach my brothers' room.
Layers of paint from 1910, shades of '50s stippling,
strips of '60s Contact paper—all eventually yielded
to a score of wallpapered years till now.
And now
I unplug the mantle clock,
for this family, in this place,
time has run out.
I turn the key for the last time,
walk to my car past my brother, crying
like the boy he once was, and we drive away slow,
a procession of packed cars, my mother in the lead
with me. She is coming to my house.

Dry-eyed, she looks straight ahead
as we leave the block where English
is no longer spoken.
She says only, "Goodbye, my life."

CARETAKER

The bell clangs its iron tongue
through a winter sunrise like dark pearls,
moths cling to cobwebs stiff from last night's sleet,
and she moves through morning,
seeing the silver streaks in the antique mirror;
time rests like a watermark on her day
skin thins and the slender tenderness of knees
so always she wears jeans and sweatshirts:
daughter of sweatshops and old textiles

the heaviness of snow clouds oppresses
her shoulders slump with their weight
trapped
(the word inadmissible)
and face-to-face with insularity, rosaries and tenements
living here now in her century-old mother

What bread shall she bake today?
What bones shall she break today?
Laundry waits, the smell of night sweats
trapped in old clothes
waiting lists of ingredients and appointments
the trash of stale words like crumbs
swept up in black plastic bags
trapped
(inadmissible)
her face in gaunt denial, but
love offered, spendthrift—
spent
and spent again.

MOTHER AND DAUGHTER

At my desk in the work room
I am content to let the landscape fail;
the house continue on in disrepair
as I sit in heavy silence.
At my late brother's house in the country
deer leap, vanishing into a dusky fog.
His dead wife's flowers
rise untended from the damp earth.
Here, on the trees, buds like small tight fists,
and the insistent rain smacking on the porch roof
like wet leaves.
          A match strikes;
guilty, I inhale
the cigarette I have given up again
and again, and for a moment I am cheered.

***
In another room, my mother
at ninety-one, sits in a stillness so deep
it is hard to tell
whether it be the stillness of prayer
or the stillness of death.
Unable now to read, she stares
at the tv's flickering images;
she is deaf, but cannot bother now with close-
captioning.
She cannot apprehend
a world where the young die first
how or why the heavy grace of God
has brought her to this place,
unwilling survivor,
purveyor of all she has lost: husband, home,

son, daughter, sister.
She asks, "What's for supper?"
and together we fill the house
with the silent burden of our grief.

New England Reincarnation

The day's temper is determined by the weather.
The benign chingk and clangk of mast lines in a sunny breeze
can swiftly shift to haunting sounds of splintering wood
the screech of tearing, twisting metal when the wind
whips out of the Northeast. The ocean loses its illusion
of inviting weightless venue for sport, and becomes
at once foreboding, menacing, with violent moods
capricious and threatening as a god's.
And I have been here before: my knowledge of this
milieu runs deep and certain,
and I felt the crush of waves
the iciness at my lower limbs, the taste of salt in my mouth
its sting in my eyes so that I cannot tell the tears,
its sticky, clinging insistent intrusion into every pore.
My floating hair changes into kelp. Waves of disembodied voices
sound the cries of the drowning, the gulls mourners
keening into the wind. When my bloated body is dredged up
the salt has sealed my lips, crusted on my lids and lashes
and my marrow has turned to ice. I know I will never know
true warmth again. Sailor on the *Argo* or beggar in *Titanic's* steerage
the memory is the same. Thus the price of knowing
the cost of consequence of unearned truth prematurely learned.
I tell you this: I taste my salted blood, and every gray day in wind,

every raw and howling night this assaulted body lives to
die again.

*The hand knit fishermen's sweaters served a purpose
more solemn than warmth: bodies found after a time at
sea could only thus be identified by each mother/sister/
lover's unique stitch.
Thus do clothes make the man.

THE LABORATORY

for my brother, Charles

I dreamed of dreaming
in our mother's house, of
poking holes in the plaster wall
separating my bedroom from my brothers'

where you grew blue crystals in petri dishes
and dissected mail-order frogs and fish
that arrived sealed in formaldehyde.
We spent our allowance on test tubes
and quarter jars of pretty chemicals.

Now the old house is emptying
like a bottle rocking on its side,
spilling its life into this artificial landscape
where the difference between recording
and reliving
is a blurred line stroked in the dark.
Smudged thoughts fly upward like startled birds,
hang in the cluttered air,
waft down to the worn rag rug.

I am dancing with scarecrows.

We share the bottle, the experiments,
the inarticulate dreams of dark rooms and cellars:
this wastebasket bulges
with the crumpled signs of distress.
And if I call you long distance,
the connection will be clear.

THE GARDEN

On white hot afternoons
the child-sized enameled tub
was our pool, filled
with cool water and
set in the shade of the tenement
in the spare quarter-acre
of our back yard.
At the opposite side in bright sun
grew the bush with purpling red raspberries
and in the square of my grandmother's garden
leaned the baking stalks of green beans,
the dusty warm leaves of tomato plants,
pale lettuce, evolving cucumbers,
half the perimeter splashes of color
in blooming marigolds, dahlias, impatiens.
I can almost see you stooped
plucking weeds.

When you watered the plants the sun made rainbows
between the garden and the tub, your feet padding in
the dirt
where push broom roads were made for matchbox cars.

      You lived
just shy of a hundred years.
      You are in your garden.
There is dust again between us.

RAG RUGS

A song, perhaps the green blues
with the rain and the grass and the sea in it;
scraps of the immigrant's life,
of seven children orphaned young;
a few years of school and then, of course, the mill—
all here, in these pieces of rag,
transformed by Granny into multi-colored rugs,
her twisted fingers tugging, teasing beauty out of scraps
weaving the poor man's Oriental—she wove the times
when the threadbare soul was worn into numbness,
when a bowl of warm milk and bits of bread spread
with molasses
was the only fare, and into the blacks she wove her grief
for a daughter lost at fourteen; the changing seasons,
the reds and oranges of New England,
or a homey checkerboard pattern from worn-through
pot holders—
every scrap had its use.
I have one of the last, its borders now unraveling. Each
morning
I pick up a newly separated bit of cloth and wonder
what piece of her life
I hold in my hands.

SOME WOMEN

Some women are a coffee house in December,
sponsoring open competition after shocks
of warm touches on the shoulder.
Someone with a city college profile teaches
how lilting it is depressed and floating,
and this one with jaw-jutting determination tries to
be everywhere at once,
bring up her children right, but cannot, of course,
offers a new hypertension, recent visitors
and literary traditions, prefers fairy tales,
yard sales and bargains, always has an apron and a lap.
Another
collects angels in any medium
rococo, Byzantine or simple as plump pumpkins
and she desperately records the minutiae of her life
snug against the traumas and daily lucidity
of a keen mind too aware of its own time passing.
One, a nun, had studied ballet and danced,
I'm told, around the darkened convent halls
at night with a late fire,
and all the old ones plain as a country wife's clothes
sometimes calico, tiny flowers on faded cotton, nylons
rolled at the knee, make tea in small pantries.

Where are you among those vulnerable and fixed stars?
Are you taking a slow walk toward your bed at night
in a stuffy city house with clocks ticking,
or the one reliving daily the once or twice
when those eyes sought your soul and grounded it
to earth and heaven both? And will you stay
long enough to learn the long way home?

None gives in to her fears, just swallows
disappointments like cough drops, reels among storms
listening to wind chimes, or a chorus
of young strong voices harmonizing,
the lump in her throat the only indication
of an innocence she knows she never owned.

THAT TIME UNDER THE WINTER MOON

for Jimmy M.

That time under the winter moon
all we did was hold hands
and skate across a frozen lake
with ice chips scattered in the sky
past the summer cottages,
site of family songs on summer porches
around the current near the bridge
where the water never freezes

I knew even then that this place
a thousand miles from home
the silence broken only by the scraping of our blades
the white blooms of our breath
heightened everything I felt
the sharp smell of the ice
of leather and wool
the cheek parentheses of your smile
the air snapping in my lungs
the eerie off-shoot lake-wide crack and moan
of water freezing and adjusting
to a solid way of life

But I did not know then
that a day would come
when I would need it all again
want to hold it in my palm
like a snow globe, to shake it just to watch
the thick flakes fall on the two skaters
only holding hands on the timeless ice
your face as it was then—the strong jaw,

the kind eyes, the broad smile—I
would need it for a place without innocence
a place under a circus moon
where ice is only what I put in drinks
and on winter days my breath is jagged
raw in my lungs, my skates just a dusty memory
hanging on the garage wall.

TRANSITION

(—with a nod to GM Hopkins)

It is as if they know
their time is short, so
this September evening
the crickets and peepers, giving
it their all, sing to the start
of the dying season, the heart's
yearning, as when the new young teen
sitting alone on the backyard swing,
learns—sudden and sharp—
a new kind of loneliness, deep
within her sex but abstract as water
a pure pain that has no color
—she has not yet learned the name
of this solitary awakening
in the song of the crickets and peepers
the beginning of an end, griever
alone and sighing in the backyard swing

PROSPECTING

for Elaine

If the breeze billows through
your summer window
and sets the lacy panels flowing
sun caught in pale filigree
patterns on golden hardwood floors,
glinting in the sheen of your grand piano,
is it a sign?
What is this wise gold
teasing those longing for love or just
surcease from pain?

We dig deep for the buried good
beneath the stories and lies
the wildflowers and weeds around the fringes
under dank basement floors
and into the moist dark earth
for the one green shoot amid the rank.

I begin my search amid this shining:
sun slants across your eyes
like two green ponds in late afternoon
light;
fills this round, plump hour
eclipsing the ancestral unease
of the coming night.

REPRIEVES

      —that 70° day in middle March
smell of lilacs, the benign
lump
      the numb relief of low numbers
—or high, depending
on the point of measure—
      that time
of the deer
crowded just outside your window, or
the sudden shimmer in your husband's eyes
at twenty-five, returning now and still
a full thirty
years later, and this:
      Today
the day began, the trees
sprang buds,
      and you are here
to bear witness.

REMISSION'S END

      When the fox barks out
I am at my porch desk
working by a window
open to the summer night:
      It is a screech with teeth in it, something
out of time and place, not this twenty-first century
world—a pterodactyl, perhaps, something monstrous
with wings. Again
      the fox barks out, much closer now,
and every hair on my forearms rises up:
         beyond this giant maple I see its slender form
         gliding low to the ground—no wings—
         but a long and vicious snout, real as the bushes
         it disappears into.
            The crickets cease their chatter
the peepers' song goes quiet, and into the silence
this once-perfect summer night
a dog howls in fright and I wait (is it mad?),
         for the fox to screech again
         as it surely will, closer,
         perhaps at the window
         I wait,
knowing that it comes
for me.

TWELVE STATIONS OF BRAIN RADIATION

This clamp at the temple
of the holy spirit
Fit the cage snugly
a crown of thorns in stainless steel
braces down on her bony shoulders
Tighten the screws
it almost brings her to her knees
clasping the hand of her friend
imagine, imagine her beach
their boat resting gently at anchor
Now the second clamp
a halo over her bald head
a sudden in-suck of breath
a tear from dim eyes
trickles down her gaunt cheek
It will all be over soon
: two empty Adirondack chairs
face the ocean at sunset
Hang in there
brace across her forehead
it will buy time, ice cold
and intricate as snowflakes
no two seconds alike in their agony
the machine hums
radiation lasers in
and the ocean stretches out
vast and indifferent
but how they loved it so
another tear spills from the well
beneath those darkened eyes
It's over now
and her body trembles

with violent relief
mercy takes its time
Brain cells shift
cancer cells shrink
or re-arrange themselves
into new complex designs.
The ocean waves rush in
to meet her.
   Can you walk?
Only on water.

WIND ADVISORY

FOR CH

All day, wind
gusting to sixty
bending ancient trees to its will.
The house trembles and it wails
around windows and doorframes
infuriated not to gain entry.
It sucks light out of day
so that I turn on all the lamps
and, just in case, the hurricane lanterns.
It flattens the grass over old graves,
and over new ones it whips away the flowers
leaves plants in tatters. I realize
I do not know where you are buried.

After hours of solitude in wind
it begins to speak in a crooning, sing-song voice.
I turn on my music.
When the power gives out, the cold creeps in
my fingertips numb, insensate,
and I know I will never feel you again.
The mind gets caught up in powerful eddies
in the wind's trash-talking rap. It says
you are dead to me now.
The torch flickers.
Outside my broad window
snow slides across the frozen harbor.

The night's deep secrets
swirl in a whirlwind.
Boughs break.

The long night looms:
The wind.
The hard freeze.
The impenetrable dark.

PHOENIX NAPPING IN WINTER

Snow pours down like a silent rain
gathering in all corners of frozen ground
blanketing the dead brown
blanket of leaves, and into this quiet the strain

of plows rumbling like thunder
banking the snow higher and higher
trapped, you build a fire
and lulled by heat and snow, curled under

fleece, you sink deep into sleep
where the place that cradled you is burning
the entire twentieth century highway turning
into an astigmatic blur, and in your deep

unconscious, your parents' words like spikes
on a polygraph telling you in their fashion
again of your guilt, and their compassion
reserved for others—your whole frangible world like

some crystal snow globe where snowfalls
on a fire, but the fire re-kindles, snapping,
over and over. And while you are napping
the snow builds up in the long halls

of sleep, deeper and deeper
till the fire is embers

and you have turned to ash.

EPIPHANY ON A CIRCUS MOON

All the way to Provincetown
the new ring glinted in the sun,
her hand feeling heavy with it.
Behind the wheel her new husband sat
in silence. She thought, *I will wake to this man
every morning*, and was content.

At Ciro and Sal's, where he knew the maitre d',
she dined on veal Marsala, glowing with champagne,
her ring catching the candlelight. They were joined
by his friends and one of his ex-wives.

After dinner, a show. He would take her
to the Crown and Anchor, where a Viking-
capped-woman-hating-piano-playing comic
had what her husband said was a very funny schtick—
the Viking chose audience victims
for a public dressing-down. Her husband sat her
in the front row and was not disappointed:
she was chosen right away, and from nose to dress
to threats of bull dykes the humiliation went on,
the husband's raucous laughter loudest in the room.

At night he did not seem to mind
her mood was not for sex.
She lay on her side, looking out the window
at the August circus moon and thought
*I will wake to this man
every morning.*

ON THE VERGE OF DIVORCE: POSTCARDS FROM NORTH TRURO

1.
Saw a schooner full rigged
riding a horizon of luminous white
sculpted clouds scud across P-town,
tender breezes lifting curtains
waft across your inert form.
At dusk, rigging stripped,
she dropped anchor
snagging the heart of the matter
taking hold, as night fell,
like an unexamined truth.

2.
Morning after rain
air heavy and thick with midges
unseen placid waves flop at the shore
tide making a desultory effort to rise.
In this fog we navigate the day
by sonar—words
bounce off bodies and walls
muted as the fog horn,
sending its long warning
into the void. We strain
for echoes, circle, retreat
insubstantial as a dream
half-recalled in morning.
Head thrums
and the wind waits like a held breath.

3.
Broom-swept sky
breeze brings the ping ping volley
of the wind chimes.
Saw the schooner,
heading north to open waters.
Begged the question.
No reply.

OWNERSHIP

Some women do not learn till middle age
that the shadow we so feared in those dark bushes—
that formless, moving, changing shape—
was our own.
What is to fear is not
some stranger
man or woman
intent on harm, but the arms
squeezing shut the sides of the ribcage
or the hands compressing the skull at the temples
or even the breath-stopping force of a fist to the lower
abdomen
—these we somehow manage
to inflict upon ourselves in virtual reality,
our defenses sometimes even causing our own demise.
We have been well trained
to take this punishment
with us, to own it fiercely,
to never give it back.
Unless, of course,
we go forward with divorce and write it all
into the final decree: I give my consent
for you to have full custody of this anger;
own your own resentment. Incapable of support,
you owe me nothing. I'll take on the house,
the kids, this life, if you'll take—off
just take off.
And take the damn bushes with you.

ORDINARY DAYS

A blank column headed Remember To.
Remember To what? Pay the bills? Attend meetings?
The column stares, demands response.
Do I dare to remember the ordinary?
This day (how long ago?)
The music of dishes being washed
and dried in harmony.
This day, this ordinary day,
the clatter of seven suppers, table chatter
amid the pungent smells of cucumbers in vinegar
onions and tender chops, a light breeze wafting
through kitchen windows of the tenement.
And after the requisite hour,
a late swim at the beach by the mill,
sun chased down by a honeydew moon
and the first star. We were rapt, wrapped shivering
in hooded terrycloth robes, and the end
of this ordinary day is blessed by crickets,
peepers, and the impossibility of a billion stars.

If this day I remember to honor my parents,
my brothers and my sister,
each hour in this finite clock is spent with voices
raised and raucous or quiet with blue notes,
secrets tight within our chests
of cardboard drawers, the bitter with the sweet,
common as cobwebs.
Upstairs the commotion:
it is Granny, dancing alone
to a Lawrence Welk waltz.

If this day I remember to grieve
the body of my mother lying above the frozen open
earth,
I weep, for you would not be warm again,
and we sang at the altar of your sacrifice.

I have loved you all with the ferocity of wolves,
howling at each headstone.

Today is an ordinary day,
the smell of cucumbers
the long songs
the night's soft sea.

THE PHOTOGRAPHER

I didn't know you
until I watched you work
cascades
an electric current
shooting through neurons
to belly to sex
      When you photograph the sea
your voice is like wind chimes on the breeze
your cap turned backwards to keep your hair
from blowing across your vision
      When your subject is a person you gaze
into the eye and you are fluidly still
energy coursing around you
like an electromagnetic field
cajoling your subject into ease
paddling gentle talk around her
inch by inch becoming her self
      How amazing to watch
those bright masks dropping away in revelation.
You are artist, magician
the essence shows her face
beguiling and true,
and in a nanosecond you trigger the net
that falls on the unsuspecting soul
captured now in the magic of your camera box.
      Erotic in the dance
between you and your equipment
extension of your sensuality
you spread the legs of your tripod
insert a wondrous filter
to show what cannot be seen
through the naked eye, gently

so gently, adjusting the exposure
coaxing the camera with the pressure of your thumb—
it was, once upon an imprint, love.

MEMORIAL

Your beauty and your vision
      were our angst. Now
the pipes and harp keen for you.
Their song rides the wind from Bray to Aran.

Go to where the storm can play itself out
      against your swollen bones
where the waves will bow to the rift
of your silent cry.
Allow the stones
to pull the pain back
let it fill the crags of cliffs.

Your blood pounds rich and thick
as the pulse and the pace of the sea:
      take your sorrow there

and tomorrow I will build you a cairn
made of marble cut from the heart
      with exquisite care.

AT THE MET, ONCE

Sculpture fragment
two fingers frozen together
touching her absent heart
the torso still remembers the whole
the silent Aegean in the aqua distance
and a stillness at the core so deep—
Now
she stands in the super supermarket
peas to her right, rice to her left,
specials at the endcaps
abundance of plastic and tin
remembering that scrap at the Met
the stone cold and alive with fluid motion
here the art of styrofoam packaging
likely to survive for generations
while all the rest is disposable
and there among the tinned vegetables
she feels the burden of grief
a blue light special
now for sale in Aisle Two.

LION IN WINTER
He waits on the windowsill, watching me
with that sidelong look that cats perfected, patient
as I finish my cigarette. Behind him, snow flies yet again
but he has lost interest in the insistent squall; we are both
impatient for spring.
The second the ash is out, he bounds on the desk
rubbing against my shoulder and writing arm, fluid as oil,
circling my work back and forth
across the book I am trying to read, the pad I am trying to write on,
circles, paces, rubs, purring loud to get my attention
then flings himself down in the middle of it all, stopping me mid-syllable
and wraps his paws around my arm. He rests his chin in my palm
drooling with delight, and his claws knead my shirt.
He is my lion in miniature.
He chuffs as I rub his tender ears and gently scrub his pure white neck
and he closes his eyes in ecstasy. I rest my face on top of his head
feeling the vibrations, and for a peaceful while we stay like that.
My work, interrupted for his pleasure, can wait
as I cast aside the weight of facts, the lonely snow, the recent loss.

Abruptly the purring stops, the tip of his long tail flicks,
claws spring out and he grips my sleeve and bites my hand, hard.
He lashes out and swipes across my cheek open-clawed,

and with an angry parting glance, launches out the
door.

He is my lion
and clearly has had enough of weakness.
Spurned, I turn back to empty words, marginalia,
the blank, unyielding canvas,
the frozen loneliness of two-dimensional surfaces.

LA FINCA CARIBE

Rain riots on the tin roof
a gecko runs the ring
around the mosquito netting
the cancerous mutt
pads to where he senses food
and the cats mewl and mewl
as if I might produce for them
several small fresh fish.

Such miracles have been known to happen
especially on this island
where hurts heal
and nightmares turn to dreams
where turquoise, aqua, jade and teal
are the colors of the day
to steal your pain and send it
floating on the trade winds.

Of course it's not that easy.
You may have to sweat a bit
deal with sand in your skin
or water trapped in your ear
so everything you hear swooshes
and sounds so low, so slow—

But you have handled worse before,
when writing meant dragging each line
a lobsterman pulling up his pots
never knowing till they surface
if they would be empty
or the catch too immature;
and you have been under the deluge,

watched snakes rattle at your feet,
found the stone bowl dry—
oh yes, you have been there
where all the world was underwater,
stared at the sightless eyes of the dead,
heard black blood whispering through paper veins
seen Hopkins' cliffs of fall in the dark
felt the stark wonder that the sun still rises
with or without you.

Coming from that to this:
it may not be loaves and fish
but it's miracle enough,
and all the palms applaud.

BONES

We walk the shoreline
with our tough bodies and soft minds
and face the righteousness of shells
bone forming smooth whorls, a bony spine
stripes of frozen sand in burnt sienna
the sea is the collective consciousness
moving among the bones, iridescent
and we wade in laughing at our nervousness
and stand, anchored by wave-thrust sand,
our bodies swaying like catechists.
This is not a baptism—I'm not saying that.
But we commingle with the souls
admire their bones
I thrust one deep in my pocket
my talisman
to ward off the devils
of dry land.

CLOSING CALL

A young native clops by on a thin grey horse
spitting his commentary into the rutted street

lined with bars and diners
with each spill the glass grows lighter

he comes, he goes,
fugitive as memory

the *touristas* sit at the bar
tended by the woman with the mohawk

one tries to capture spilt mercury
from a broken thermometer

and nothing is more dangerous
than a glass about to be emptied.

Closing call. The horseman clip clops
into the dim east end.

SOUVENIRS

Seawater foams into the bluff, slams against stones,
etches new paths in the corrugated heart. Sun the color
of beach plums
goes down,
goes down. She scans the bay
squint-eyed, as if each new wave

would bring the errant traveler home. A host
of stars winking overhead promise
confidences, undercurrents whisper into the salt air,
her dark secrets floating out where no one ever hears.

When the world in morning tilts, tidal flats stretch
like corduroy, wrinkling almost to the wreck
of the *James Longstreet*, the jagged rusted halves
housing
unexploded munitions. Mussel shells, razor clams,
writhing

periwinkles punctuate the wet sand and a black-backed
gull
swoops, snatches something dark and small
and alive, then reels off triumphant in wind.
Stranded sailfish, sunfish, beetle cats, toys of old
children

lay scattered across the flats. Dressed in day-glo green
and orange
children float kites like red diamonds
letting out line, careful not to let the tether go.
A dark woman wanders where the ocean flow

skims her ankles. She sings
scales into the ebb tide breeze, flung notes rising
and falling with the air currents.
The watcher on the flats

catches them in nets like silver minnows,
gathers slipper shells and conches, a pocketful
of skipping stones,
the wistful fragments of yesterday's songs.

BEAUTY

For Abe Landau, at Auschwitz

Despite the objective datum of the clock
the stark darkness of nightmares
descends yet again:
rusted tin soldiers beat you
hold your backside to the stove fire
blistering the price you paid
for bartered bread.

Do you recall envying a frog in the pond
its freedom to splash away? You, too,
would sate your hunger with insects.

Still, you mention this or that day
was beautiful, and in a moment of lucidity
sun thawed your frozen soul
echoing a life many worlds away.

Is that what sustained you—
a flower daring to rise up from mud
boldly beautiful even crushed under jackboots?
You dared to love the matted petals
while transports came thousands full
and chuffed away empty,
remnants collected for Canada.

And still you can say a day is beautiful
even as your belly twisted,
even as your shadow all but disappeared.

LADYBUGS

Ladybugs crawl indoors and gather in groups
gossiping in the corner of the room of new snow.
They know; it's programmed in their genes
and the weatherman bears them out:
another six inches expected this night.
She lights a fire in the empty house.
How can they know, these wee dots of black on red,
what maps cannot tell?

In their own homes her children gather with friends
trade gossip, revel in the storm.

She dusts their pictures lining the wall,
a sigh rising like chimney smoke
from the fire they were born in.

It is as it should be:
the ladybugs, the winter, this snow
and all the children gone.

The feral black cat

moves in shadow
sleek and supremely indifferent
even to bribes of chopped meat.
I do not need you, she meows,
so why are you looking?
Why go to such extents
just to stroke my fur?
She stares with yellow eyes
then moves on, the white spats
on her paws disembodied in darkness
tapping across the floorboards
leaving behind
all the day's disappointments
and a hand
outstretched.

POETRY READING

for Donald Hall

The aging poet leaves the podium
unsteady but proudly unaided
showing art's ravenous attachment
to life, and though he spoke of death
he is stronger in the broken places
and snow dissolves into peonies
the bleating of lambs
the pungent sweet smells
of the drying hay.

PEACHES

She is a beautiful girl
not yet twenty-one
sitting with her grandmother.
It is late summer
but fall winds have blown in
heralding the remnants
of a dying hurricane
blowing itself out on landfall.
Trees bow and sway
talking, talking
in their weather dance.
The grandmother carefully (even tenderly)
has dried and crushed the pits
of peaches, hard and under-ripe:
the cyanide powder waits
powerfully frozen in the fridge
between the chops and the chicken tenders.
This will be your last job for me
she tells the girl
soon to be a woman,
the MRI in green and black
and terrible silent white
does not lie.
Into the flailing, gossiping trees
she says
just feed me
when it's time.

PAINTING A POEM

At first, lassitude. Then a layer of gesso,
a layer of titanium white. Work in
cerulean If it's a happy poem. No?
Then Prussian blue will do.
Clouds amass in sky and neutral greys.
Is there no hope?
Ah, yes: a lighthouse,
beam bone bright, warm, glowing
cool colors for dunes and shade.
The sea is rough: more Prussian,
more titanium for the whitecaps.
Is there drama?
Yes, a boat, a curragh
tossed among the waves,
a rocky shoal.
Tension?
Yes: the curragh, manned by two young boys
will never make it home.
Their oars are like matchsticks
against the frothy sea.
You can see that they are destined
to fight the waves forever,
but their arms are as thin as stick figures.
Their parents will be worried sick.
Their boys are lost, forever,
for in the next stanza,
the next canvas, up close
pulling in the curragh
they are men
with lined and weathered faces
no traces of the boys
who had set out that morning.

IN MY CHILDHOOD

The shadow of the squat cottage
begins to pull into itself
we are in the remains
of another summer weekend
between the deadfall and the stumps
the outhouse, scrub pine and sedge bush
between the mill and the lake
the color of strong brewed tea
and hoarhound drops
when the sun goes down
and time hurtles us forward
the sun sets early on us all
and we are left to cope
with the greying day
in whatever way we can
Soon it will be fall.
The children play hide and seek
until mosquitoes drive them in
they sit on the porch among
the high black shoes, the feet
of the old people
and learn their songs
in the dark harmonies
that will carry them like fathers
when they are drowsy
and soft in their extra-large sweatshirts and worn
denim
into the car
into
the next century

INSOMNIA

A heavy-lidded glance shows the time:
my three-fifteen a.m. date with the clock
continues. We have been meeting now for months
to pass the time.

I sat for an hour wearing sunglasses in the darkness
of the dining room. Last week
I put a bowl of ice cream out for my dead mother.
Sometimes, I work a *Times* crossword puzzle

too afraid to sleep
to meet the dizzying images of lost keys,
foreign cars, and unfamiliar streets. The sheets smother.
There is no reprieve from time

the wind chimes hanging from the maple's limb
clang the passing minutes as they turn to hours
and somewhere far away a foghorn moans
and that tide of old times dashes in

clashing with the wind, splashing over the flat stones
of the jetty. Those factories still left
come alive with the next shift:
machines hum, rumble and clank. In time,

strangers in an old tenement rise to a new heat
the ghosts of my family hovering in the woodwork.
The windows still rattle on their broken ropes
and the cellar's just as musty with time and stale air,

secrets, and the stuff of nightmares.
Sky lightens. We have survived the limitless vocabulary

of the dark, another desperate trip down unlit roads
where time takes its painstaking time, passing.

KATRINKA

Part Two

PEDOPHILIA

One pays dearly
for lacking the courage of beatified girls
—those sainted faces painted with smug innocence—
for exchanging martyrdom and sure heaven
for pocketsful of small change
      jangling of guilt and shame

For those who do not opt
for death, the rest
      will have to wait.
      We are busy
cringing from raucous laughter
scrambling after fragments
      to puzzle into a fractured integrity
for the stale crusts of love flung across the floor.
      We are busy
taking control wherever we can find it
hammering brass vases and filling them
      with dandelions and purple weeds collected
roadside

Blessed are the violated young
for they shall inherit the dust.

KATRINKA AND THE APPLE

It was nothing personal,
you understand,
this moment of her imperfect blooming
immense indifference scratching at the pane
through dust-filtered light
in musty cellars against the whitewashed walls.
Trees fall. Waves crash. Children hide
in the hollows eating stolen apples
poisoned with their shame.

KATRINKA'S FAMILY

What murderers, what skeletons
in this closet? None. Only . . .
Breath whispers against wool coats,
slides down the linings,
and silences like liquid silks,
a faint rustle against drycleaner bags
now and then . . . there is nothing
to report here, no seedy scandal,
spies or intrigue; just a little
trouble
is all, and *everyone*
has some of that

stashed away in aromatic cedar chests
layered among the lace doilies
and the Christening gowns
wrapped in yellowed tissue paper
that cannot bear
the glare of public scrutiny.
They simply know what not to see.
They are discreet
in what they hear.

KATRINKA IN THERAPY

A thought might grow here
if planted
just so, sprout
between loose stones, perhaps,
and rise triumphant,
a nacreous tribute
to the tireless tender
of the garden.

On the other hand,
should rock completely cover land,
would thought become ingrown,
its roots so tangled with neurons
as to give synapses pause?
If speechless pain be the inverse of thought,
who will tend the mute?

ALL THINGS START IN THE BEDROOM

where Katrinka was always lonely
and nightly battled insomnia, especially
since the sister she shared room and bed with
had abandoned her for college far away.
She was eight.
Some nights she occupied her time
digging a hole through the plaster wall
to break through to the room
where her three brothers slept. Some nights
she sang every song she knew
until the aunt came upstairs and screamed
     Turn your face to the wall
     and go to sleep!
and shut the door. Katrinka hated
the dark. Other nights
the uncle came up, but he had
his own agenda and certainly did not
want her to be asleep. The best nights
were when she would beg her father
to come and lie down with her,
just for a little while
and he'd give in. He was instantly
asleep and she took care of him,
covering his tired legs with the extra blanket,
burrowing against his back,
feeling the softness of his thin tee shirt,
smelling his man-smell, a mixture
of the mill and the bar
warm and this night safe
proud
that her father protected her—
even if he didn't know it.

KATRINKA: A BIOGRAPHY

She seeks validation
wherever she can find it
no one had told her
she was a girl
only what she was not
a boy, for instance,
never innocent an instant
they made her guilty on her birth day
practicing their maleness
on her unsuspecting body
and she found her usefulness there.
She grew in fear
of strangers in the bushes
lurking in the dark branches
of her tangled imagination.

At four she ran away
peddling her tricycle
with spindly legs
the strangers that she met
had been kind, helping her across
the busy streets.
She was seven
long blocks from home when found
and they carried her back
inarticulate as a yowl.

The trajectory of pain spans fifty years
the mystery of numbness
time passing on strings that measure nanoseconds
the membrane to the mind's museum
those moments of torment

still fragile. She touches them
in her isolation: she owns them

and a solitary life.

KATRINKA CONSIDERS FAITH

She wants to let loose
a torrent, unspeakable words,
in madness to recapture
all of that spirit that
   spirited away
when she wasn't looking—
she stares at the night sky
her fists clenched like spring buds
   just before the rain that frees them
as if all the dead could shake up the stars
to comprehensible shapes, or to take
one bright light and fling it
   across the arcing universe
—even then she would find some way
to mistrust her own eyes
and all those distant stars
were just rigid points
   in pointless space.
The ugly child didn't know
what to believe
since, not one of the blessed
who trusts without sight,
she's an unholy creature
who's tethered to earth
astonished by stars,
her vain belief a shallow-rooted thing
in the company of worms.

KATRINKA RE-ENTERS HER LIFE AT A MIDPOINT,

diving deep as the bay floor would allow
senses panic in her lungs but opens her eyes anyway.
Easing up, she sees children
playing Frisbee, their brown lithe bodies scuttling
      across the sand like hermit crabs,
sees married women sharing notes on operations, sales,
best sellers,
sees their men relaxing with novels, or watching.
      And they are all so easy in their skin,
confident even in their dilemmas.
It is she who is the stranger;
it is they who crowd the shallows.

But even in imagination is disconnection,
and the fog rolls up from the sea right into her eyes
and hangs there, calm and quiet-like,
until she feels the appalling weight of her limbs,
the striated flesh of her torso,
anchored to a separateness
no touch but any in passing,
could look but never see beyond the fog
of her own design.

Back on deck she wonders idly which will go first
(heart? lungs?) And why her clothes never seem to
belong to her.
She fantasizes a lover, someone not cowed by this
immensity of sky,
who would recognize the pounding waves
for the anger that they are
and navigate beneath them.

KATRINKA'S PREDATOR

You basked in the pure light
of children's trust.
How did it feel to take those
      slender, tender arms
and crush them beneath the weight
of your desire?
When you finished—when you were done—
sated
did you could you look at those small bodies
and see your ruin there?
Did you dare to lower your eyes to theirs,
to read the confusion, anger, shame
you with your adult stature spilled into them?
It was no doubt nothing personal. Why
you *loved* them, after all, how
could love be poison?
I marvel at the power sheer and full
to claim not just this innocence here and now
but all those futures—imagine!—
Forever tainted, forever contaminated
by the toxin of your touch.
How few the actions we can daily take
that still will resonate years from now. But yours?
How terrible the power that every child
to come before your bench
left shackled in shame
with a life sentence.

KATRINKA: SURVIVOR

Clouds like windblown smoke
wisp across the white disk
of the risen sun. the streets
are empty, bare; the town still sleeps
unaware of its sins. But one girl lies
awake, taking them all in, spinning
with the centrifugal force field
of guilt, sucking them up
without discrimination.
Smooth and worn as beach glass,
the jagged edges of her wrongs
and when she sleeps, she sleeps alone
with her nightmare visions
knowing that, for her, love
is not an option—the most
she expects is contempt
or the immense indifference of a remorseless sun,
casting her in the shadows
of her immutable guilt.

KATRINKA AT 50

Leave her to her music,
let her reconstruct the sustaining dream
where all her contradictions make sense
and all the guilt and sins—
committed, omitted, contemplated—
are master-quilted into a single seamless sail

and sail her home to watch the oak leaves
warm to gold in the changing green of the autumn
breeze
her mood fluttering like the wind sock
somewhere between New Bedford and Nantucket,
textile mills and ivied halls,
Miller and Mozart, King and Coltrane
changeable as the shoreline
where Mrs. Townley taught the shivering bunch of
them
how to float acceptably as dead men.

Let her tack through the ancient harbor full
of ghost ships and Ahab, and smell
in the redolent air the distant scents of summer
alive again in the horseshoe crabs,
a fishing pole made of bamboo and string
with a wicked hook for wiggly-boy worms.

There are strangers in her tenement house.

But the lakeside cottage still stands, where they had
Ivory soap baths in the lake, caught a bucketful
of hornpouts, raced penny turtles they kept in a pail of
brown water

and they sat at the feet of the old people
on the porch when the sun went down
and they listened to sounds of their stories and songs
(It's the ripple effect of a pebble tossed into the water
with a wish.)

Let her be spendthrift with time
and squander her hopes on each of these pure
and unalterable notes.

APOLOGIA PRO VITA MEA

A child survivor's guilt
A child, she had no right to speak; silence
of the insides became her milieu.
"Secretive," they said. So for years
she only sang and told her sad little tales
through the safety of others' songs and fears
until a minor-key surgery destroyed those four-part
chords.
Would there be nothing now, all those notes
plumbed from her soul forever lost?
When they began to call her "It" instead
of her name, she made a friend of whole cloth
and called him Biddle. He let her talk
so she would not forget how. But when
she spoke of sin, he fled,
not wanting to be in on it. Then
they taught her the finer points of cruelty—she would
not cry—
and the man downstairs taught her pleasures
no child should ever learn. When they heard,
they taught her shame and she broke
off from their world like a dry twig
became a god and found herself responsible
for World War II; Hiroshima was her doing.
Nowadays she lives a quiet life
with the guilt of a million deaths
and her own defeat, while civilization crumbles
at her dirty feet.

A CUP OF TREMBLING

A door closes quietly.
Footsteps approach.
She ducks behind a handmade quilt
dense poetry, blues and swirls of acrylics
literary criticism, and as a last resort
inside the cup of her own skull.
She is adept at wall flowering.
She has an affinity for cats
and rabbits.
But when she explodes
the whole world shakes
and she becomes a red balloon
the air suddenly let out
membrane flying around the room
then dropping, exhausted,
a sad little scrap
on the dusty floor.

Behind the fluttering curtain

of her once gentle sensibilities, she assembles
the pieces of her anger. Dark leaves
wet, clinging desperately to each other—
they are after all useful as mulch
for a winter garden.
Betty Crocker
Bette Davis
Betty Friedan
Her whole life a series of missed cues
as she defines herself only against another person,
thing, parent: she is only who
she is not. With backdrop of darkness
she is a child who has outgrown everything
except memory—they would have you think
that time passes by, what's done is done,
what's gone is gone.
　　　　But with memory
time collapses into a void,
and what burned yesterday returns alas
to burn again though with a different quality
of illumination lighting those dark corners
of an immutable shame.

POST SCRIPTS

Part Three

TO A NEW GENERATION

My tired eyes cannot hold you;
they ache and squint and still
I cannot hold your message
of torture in another country.
To try to take it in
is to blast the retina
and I love the life
insignificant
earth-bound in my own trap
going through the petty motions
day to day
the slow pages that turn fast
while the years pile up
like snow on snow
the legs, the voice, the grip, the go
each day another incremental loss.
So when you tell me of torture by my countrymen
how should I respond?
I did my anti-war time long ago
and have been silent ever since.
It is your time now
to hold the signs,
though in my heart
from my small room
I promise to praise your slow march
against uniforms and suits,
pray you do a better job
than we, and that in your youthful wisdom,
your vision will stay focused on a life,
unclouded by the Cause.

REDEMPTION

Hearing the dusk
the whole landscape alive
with all manner of song
orchestrated by a very large grasshopper
in a black tuxedo and a white turtleneck
an adagio for wings
legs and vocals:
each of us listening
to her own strains of heartbreak
or love
we are mute with wonder
alive
ready to stand and shout Bravo!
at the last shivering note
and the grasshopper maestro
turning toward the porch,
gives a low, dignified bow.

www.ingramcontent.com/pod-product-compliance
Lightning Source LLC
Chambersburg PA
CBHW071018040426
42443CB00007B/830